The Author's Way

The 90-Day Journey to Finding Your Voice

Jennifer Wright

Copyright © 2023 Jennifer Wright

All rights reserved. No part of this book may be reproduced, stored in a retrievable system or transmitted, in any form or by any means without prior written consent of the publisher, except in the case of brief quotations, embodied reviews and articles.

Execuwright.com

Cover Design by: Jennifer Wright

Edited and Published by The Author's Way Publishing
www.TheAuthorsWayPublishing.com
Atlanta, GA

ISBN: 979-8-9872222-4-9 (Paperback)
ISBN: 979-8-9872222-5-6 (Hardcover)

THE AUTHOR'S WAY JOURNAL

This Author's Way Journal Belongs to:

Name: _____

Phone: _____

Email: _____

THE AUTHOR'S WAY JOURNAL

Dedication

This book is dedicated to every author, published and unpublished, who wanted to do more writing but held themselves back. It is dedicated to everyone who felt they didn't have the stories or the expertise to step into their space and speak their thoughts. It's dedicated to every person who has struggled to become who they really are and share their voice.

My hope is that this journal will give you the confidence and drive to finish that book, write that article, step on that stage or just stand in your power and know that you are a writer and author, a creative who has important stories to share.

THE AUTHOR'S WAY JOURNAL

Introduction

I deeply believe that writing is a learned, creative skill that, similar to playing an instrument or learning any other skills, becomes better with practice. Great practice makes great writers and authors.

Many years ago, I had a good friend who was a musician. He played in a Latin band and in a church orchestra. Two to three times per week he played gigs. He also practiced four to five times a week. For every hour he played professionally, he practiced an average of 2 hours.

As many of you know, I am also an amateur standup comedian. Practice has become critical to being funny on stage. Every time I participate in a show, I practice my set up to 50 times. The more I practice the more confident I am when I get on stage.

Often, I hear people say, "I'm not a good writer." Or when I tell them I'm a book writer they say, "I wish I could do that." Most people are better writers than they think they are. Writing is a learned skill and no matter how good you think you are or are not, you can become better, through practice.

We spend much of our time creating content for our projects. We get frustrated when we feel our writing isn't as good as it could be. By practicing our craft regularly, the time we spend on our content projects can become more efficient and we can produce higher quality content.

This 90-day journal is created in order to help the reader to build a habit of daily writing. The prompts and writing ideas, makes it so the reader does not have to worry about what to write, they can simply start to write.

Practice can make all of the difference in the quality of your writing, how your brain processes what you write and crafting new content ideas. Practice will train your brain to start thinking differently about your writing and making you much more comfortable with yourself as a writer.

I sincerely hope that you enjoy using this journal and you are successful at whatever writing goals you have.

Enjoy!

Jennifer

THE AUTHOR'S WAY JOURNAL

How to Use This Journal

This is a 90-day journal. Each day has two pages dedicated to it. Capture the date at the top of each page in order to track how you do with your daily practice. You do not have to write for consecutive days. Don't worry if there are days you miss. If you miss a day or 2 or 20, pick up where you are and start writing again.

For each day you have several ways that you can write.

1. *Writing Prompt:* The statement at the top of the day's first page is provided to give you an idea of what to write about. You can use that statement to tell a story, write a description or free-write anything that comes to mind when you read the prompt.
2. *High Vibration Word:* Each day includes a high vibration word at the bottom of the day's first page. A high vibration word is one that has high, positive energy. High vibration words are used to help inspire, motivate and create ideas for your writing. You can use that word as a topic for your writing that day.
3. *Gratitude:* At the bottom of the day's second page, you will also see an opportunity to write what you are grateful for that day. You can

write about your gratitude that day on the day's pages.
4. *Another topic:* You can write on any other topic you choose that day. Maybe something happened that you'd like to write about or you want to write about someone new you just met. Any topic is free game.
5. *Free-write:* Free-writing is a method of writing that helps you clear your head and get thoughts out. Put pen to paper and just start writing. You can write words, phrases, sentences, streams of thought, whatever you choose is allowed.

This is your journal and your practice. You are allowed to use it in any way you like.

The pages are also created with dotted page guides. This allows you to use them to write, doodle, draw, mind map, brainstorm, or any other creative processes you would like to use.

There are several blank pages in the back of the journal. If you find that two pages is not enough for everything you want to write that day, you can use the pages in the back to complete your thoughts.

THE AUTHOR'S WAY JOURNAL

THE AUTHOR'S WAY JOURNAL

Day 1   Date: ____/____/____

Set a timer and write for 10 minutes about today. If it's the start of the day, what do you want to happen? If the end of the day, what happened?

Daily Word: Gratitude

THE AUTHOR'S WAY JOURNAL

Today I am Grateful for: _____

Day 2   Date: ____/____/____

Look around you. Find an item and write a story about it. Where did it come from? What does it mean to you or someone else in your life? How did it come to be where it is?

Daily Word: Meditation

THE AUTHOR'S WAY JOURNAL

Today I am Grateful for: _____

THE AUTHOR'S WAY JOURNAL

Day 3   Date: ____/____/____

Write a letter to a friend or family member you have not connected with in a while. Think about what you would like to share with that person.

Daily Word: Praise

THE AUTHOR'S WAY JOURNAL

Today I am Grateful for: _____

THE AUTHOR'S WAY JOURNAL

Day 4   Date: ____/____/____

Write about an experience you had from someone else's point of view.

Daily Word: Nurture

THE AUTHOR'S WAY JOURNAL

Today I am Grateful for: _____

THE AUTHOR'S WAY JOURNAL

Day 5   Date: ____/____/____

Write about a book you read as if you are giving a recommendation to a friend.

Daily Word: Action

THE AUTHOR'S WAY JOURNAL

Today I am Grateful for: _____

THE AUTHOR'S WAY JOURNAL

Day 6   Date: ____/____/____

Write about a talk you recently heard or a video you recently watched. What did you learn? What did the talk or video mean to you?

Daily Word: Acceptance

THE AUTHOR'S WAY JOURNAL

Today I am Grateful for: _____

THE AUTHOR'S WAY JOURNAL

Day 7   Date: ____/____/____

Write about the happiest day of your life. What happened that made it a happy day? Is there anything you would change about that day?

Daily Word: Prosperity

THE AUTHOR'S WAY JOURNAL

Today I am Grateful for: _____

THE AUTHOR'S WAY JOURNAL

Day 8   Date: ____/____/____

Write about yesterday.

Daily Word: Alignment

THE AUTHOR'S WAY JOURNAL

Today I am Grateful for: _____

Day 9   Date: ____/____/____

Write about a time that you felt hurt. Don't be afraid to be vulnerable.

Daily Word: Alignment

THE AUTHOR'S WAY JOURNAL

Today I am Grateful for:

THE AUTHOR'S WAY JOURNAL

Day 10   Date: ___/___/___

Describe a person who had a strong influence on your life.

Daily Word: Gratitude

THE AUTHOR'S WAY JOURNAL

Today I am Grateful for: _____

THE AUTHOR'S WAY JOURNAL

Day 11   Date: ____/____/____

Describe a person you only met once. Imagine what happened with them after they met you.

Daily Word: Integrity

THE AUTHOR'S WAY JOURNAL

Today I am Grateful for:

THE AUTHOR'S WAY JOURNAL

Day 12   Date: ____/____/____

Write about the best meal you ever had.

Daily Word: Forgiveness

THE AUTHOR'S WAY JOURNAL

Today I am Grateful for: _____

THE AUTHOR'S WAY JOURNAL

Day 13   Date: ____/____/____

Write about something you have never done as if you had.

Daily Word: Opportunity

THE AUTHOR'S WAY JOURNAL

Today I am Grateful for: _____

THE AUTHOR'S WAY JOURNAL

Day 14   Date: ____/____/____

Write about how you learned something (how you learned to drive, cook, do laundry, swim, etc.)

Daily Word: Light

THE AUTHOR'S WAY JOURNAL

Today I am Grateful for: _____

THE AUTHOR'S WAY JOURNAL

Day 15   Date: ____/____/____

Write for 10 minutes about nothing. Put pen to paper or fingers on keyboard and just start writing. Words, phrases, sentences, thoughts, ideas or just random letter. Just Write!

Daily Word: Courage

THE AUTHOR'S WAY JOURNAL

Today I am Grateful for: _____

THE AUTHOR'S WAY JOURNAL

Day 16   Date: ___/___/____

Write about your favorite thing as a child. You can describe it, share a memory about it or write about why it was or is so meaningful to you.

Daily Word: Excellence

THE AUTHOR'S WAY JOURNAL

Today I am Grateful for: _____

THE AUTHOR'S WAY JOURNAL

Day 17   Date: ____/____/____

Write about a happy time in your life. Did something specific happen? Did it involve other people? What was the ultimate outcome?

Daily Word: Grace

THE AUTHOR'S WAY JOURNAL

Today I am Grateful for: _____

THE AUTHOR'S WAY JOURNAL

Day 18   Date: ____/____/____

Write about a sad time in your life, the people, the place, the situation.

Daily Word: Generosity

THE AUTHOR'S WAY JOURNAL

Today I am Grateful for: _____

Day 19   Date: ___/___/___

Write about the person you admire the most. How do you know them? What do you admire about that person? Is there anything you would like to ask them?

Daily Word: Endearment

THE AUTHOR'S WAY JOURNAL

Today I am Grateful for: _____

THE AUTHOR'S WAY JOURNAL

Day 20　　　　　　　　　　Date: ____/____/____

Write about what you would like to be doing 10 years from now or 20 years from now. How different will your life be?

Daily Word: Remarkable

THE AUTHOR'S WAY JOURNAL

Today I am Grateful for:

THE AUTHOR'S WAY JOURNAL

Day 21   Date: ____/____/____

Think about a good friend and describe them. What makes that person such a good friend? What do you admire the most about them?

Daily Word: Sincerity

THE AUTHOR'S WAY JOURNAL

Today I am Grateful for: _____

THE AUTHOR'S WAY JOURNAL

Day 22   Date: ____/____/____

What is the bravest thing you have ever done? Share a story about it.

Daily Word: Enrichment

THE AUTHOR'S WAY JOURNAL

Today I am Grateful for:

THE AUTHOR'S WAY JOURNAL

Day 23   Date: ____/____/____

Write about an experience that makes you laugh. Describe the experience. What about it made you laugh?

Daily Word: Unconditional Love

THE AUTHOR'S WAY JOURNAL

Today I am Grateful for: _____

Day 24   Date: ____/____/____

Briefly tell someone else's story.

Daily Word: Relaxation

THE AUTHOR'S WAY JOURNAL

Today I am Grateful for: _____

Day 25 Date: ___/___/___

Have a conversation with someone you admire and share the conversation.

Daily Word: Thoughtfulness

THE AUTHOR'S WAY JOURNAL

Today I am Grateful for: _____

THE AUTHOR'S WAY JOURNAL

Day 26   Date: ____/____/____

Choose 5 or 10 words and write new definitions for each word.

Daily Word: Determination

THE AUTHOR'S WAY JOURNAL

Today I am Grateful for: _____

THE AUTHOR'S WAY JOURNAL

Day 27   Date: ___/___/___

Write about a conflict you had with someone. Was it resolved and how?

Daily Word: Mercy

THE AUTHOR'S WAY JOURNAL

Today I am Grateful for: _____

Day 28   Date: ____/____/____

Choose an object that has some special meaning from your childhood and write about it. Describe it and write about an experience you had with that object.

Daily Word: Creativity

THE AUTHOR'S WAY JOURNAL

Today I am Grateful for: _____

THE AUTHOR'S WAY JOURNAL

Day 29 	Date: ____/____/____

If you could change anything about yourself. What would it be. Why would you change it?

Daily Word: Respect

THE AUTHOR'S WAY JOURNAL

Today I am Grateful for: _____

THE AUTHOR'S WAY JOURNAL

Day 30   Date: ____/____/____

Write about your perfect day. This can be either a day that actually happened or your definition of a perfect day.

Daily Word: Honesty

THE AUTHOR'S WAY JOURNAL

Today I am Grateful for: _____

Day 31   Date: ___/___/___

Read a newspaper – either paper or online. Write about a story that you read.

Daily Word: Awareness

THE AUTHOR'S WAY JOURNAL

Today I am Grateful for: _____

THE AUTHOR'S WAY JOURNAL

Day 32 Date: ___/___/___

Write about a place you went as a child. Describe it. What did you do? What did it mean to you?

Daily Word: Mastery

THE AUTHOR'S WAY JOURNAL

Today I am Grateful for: _____

THE AUTHOR'S WAY JOURNAL

Day 33   Date: ___/___/___

If you could be anywhere in the world right now, write about what it would look like outside your window.

Daily Word: Love

THE AUTHOR'S WAY JOURNAL

Today I am Grateful for: _____

THE AUTHOR'S WAY JOURNAL

Day 34   Date: ____/____/____

Write about your name. Do you like or dislike your name? Why? What is the meaning behind your name? Where you named after someone?

Daily Word: Perseverance

THE AUTHOR'S WAY JOURNAL

Today I am Grateful for: _____

THE AUTHOR'S WAY JOURNAL

Day 35   Date: ____/____/____

Write about the worst job you ever had.

Daily Word: Self-Awareness

THE AUTHOR'S WAY JOURNAL

Today I am Grateful for: _____

Day 36   Date: ___/___/__

Write about a goal that you have. Why do you have that goal? What will it look like when you reach that goal? How will it help you or others?

Daily Word: Productivity

THE AUTHOR'S WAY JOURNAL

Today I am Grateful for: _____

THE AUTHOR'S WAY JOURNAL

Day 37   Date: ____/____/____

Rate your level of happiness today on a scale of 1-10. Write about it. What is making you as happy or as unhappy as you are?

Daily Word: Involvement

THE AUTHOR'S WAY JOURNAL

Today I am Grateful for: _____

THE AUTHOR'S WAY JOURNAL

Day 38   Date: ____/____/____

Write about your hobby or hobbies. Why do you choose those hobbies? What do they do for you?

Daily Word: Magnificent

THE AUTHOR'S WAY JOURNAL

Today I am Grateful for:

THE AUTHOR'S WAY JOURNAL

Day 39   Date: ____/____/____

What thing have you acquired that has given you the most joy?

Daily Word: Perspective

THE AUTHOR'S WAY JOURNAL

Today I am Grateful for: _____

THE AUTHOR'S WAY JOURNAL

Day 40   Date: ____/____/____

Write about the most beautiful place or thing you have ever seen.

Daily Word: Consideration

THE AUTHOR'S WAY JOURNAL

Today I am Grateful for: _____

THE AUTHOR'S WAY JOURNAL

Day 41   Date: ___/___/___

Write about your favorite job. What made it your favorite? Is it a job you still have?

Daily Word: Equality

THE AUTHOR'S WAY JOURNAL

Today I am Grateful for: _____

Day 42 Date: ____/____/____

Write about a time that you tried something new and it didn't work out. What did you try? What happened? Did you learn anything from the experience?

Daily Word: Abundance

THE AUTHOR'S WAY JOURNAL

Today I am Grateful for:

Day 43 Date: ___/___/___

Write about an adventure you had. It can be something you did as a child or as an adult. Write about the adventure or anything you learned from the experience.

Daily Word: Restoration

THE AUTHOR'S WAY JOURNAL

Today I am Grateful for:

Day 44	Date: ____/____/____

Write about the first time you lived alone or the first time you live outside of your parents' home.

Daily Word: Vitality

THE AUTHOR'S WAY JOURNAL

Today I am Grateful for: _____

THE AUTHOR'S WAY JOURNAL

Day 45 Date: ___/___/___

Kismet is destiny or when something was meant to be. Write about an experience that you had that was meant to be.

Daily Word: Tranquility

THE AUTHOR'S WAY JOURNAL

Today I am Grateful for:

THE AUTHOR'S WAY JOURNAL

Day 46   Date: ____/____/____

Write about your first time of doing something. The first time you flew. The first time you drove. The first time you went shopping on your own.

Daily Word: Valuable

THE AUTHOR'S WAY JOURNAL

Today I am Grateful for:

THE AUTHOR'S WAY JOURNAL

Day 47   Date: ____/____/____

Write about a time when everything when just as you planned.

Daily Word: Originality

THE AUTHOR'S WAY JOURNAL

Today I am Grateful for:

Day 48   Date: ____/____/____

Write about the favorite place you have traveled.

Daily Word: Ingenuity

THE AUTHOR'S WAY JOURNAL

Today I am Grateful for:

THE AUTHOR'S WAY JOURNAL

Day 49 Date: ____/____/____

Write about your largest purchase to date. What was it? How did you feel about it? Do you still own it?

Daily Word: Enlightenment

THE AUTHOR'S WAY JOURNAL

Today I am Grateful for: _____

THE AUTHOR'S WAY JOURNAL

Day 50   Date: ____/____/____

Write about a time when you gave just the right gift. What was the gift and to whom? How did it make them feel? How did it make you feel?

Daily Word: Esteem

THE AUTHOR'S WAY JOURNAL

Today I am Grateful for:

THE AUTHOR'S WAY JOURNAL

Day 51 Date: ____/____/____

Write about where you grew up.

Daily Word: Gentleness

THE AUTHOR'S WAY JOURNAL

Today I am Grateful for:

THE AUTHOR'S WAY JOURNAL

Day 52   Date: ____/____/____

Write about a time when you overcame a significant challenge.

Daily Word: Achievement

THE AUTHOR'S WAY JOURNAL

Today I am Grateful for: _____

THE AUTHOR'S WAY JOURNAL

Day 53   Date: ____/____/____

Write about something you would like to start. A new hobby, a new habit, new friends.

Daily Word: Consciousness

THE AUTHOR'S WAY JOURNAL

Today I am Grateful for: _____

Day 54   Date: ___/___/___

Write about a time when you trusted your gut or you intuition.

Daily Word: Harmony

THE AUTHOR'S WAY JOURNAL

Today I am Grateful for:

Day 55

Date: ____/____/____

Write about the biggest lesson you learned in the past 12 months. What happened that helped you to learn the lesson?

Daily Word: Motivation

THE AUTHOR'S WAY JOURNAL

Today I am Grateful for: _____

THE AUTHOR'S WAY JOURNAL

Day 56   Date: ____/____/____

Write about a memorable holiday.

Daily Word: Giving

THE AUTHOR'S WAY JOURNAL

Today I am Grateful for: _____

THE AUTHOR'S WAY JOURNAL

Day 58   Date: ____/____/____

Write about the last thing you did with a group.

Daily Word: Quietness

THE AUTHOR'S WAY JOURNAL

Today I am Grateful for: _____

THE AUTHOR'S WAY JOURNAL

Day 59 Date: ____/____/____

Write about your biggest strength.

Daily Word: Self

THE AUTHOR'S WAY JOURNAL

Today I am Grateful for: _____

THE AUTHOR'S WAY JOURNAL

Day 60   Date: ____/____/____

Write about your biggest weakness.

Daily Word: Thrive

THE AUTHOR'S WAY JOURNAL

Today I am Grateful for: _____

THE AUTHOR'S WAY JOURNAL

Day 61   Date: ____/____/____

Write about the best meal you ever had.

Daily Word: Wellbeing

THE AUTHOR'S WAY JOURNAL

Today I am Grateful for: _____

THE AUTHOR'S WAY JOURNAL

Day 62   Date: ____/____/____

Write about your least favorite food.

Daily Word: Uplifted

THE AUTHOR'S WAY JOURNAL

Today I am Grateful for: _____

THE AUTHOR'S WAY JOURNAL

Day 63 Date: ____/____/____

Have you ever quit anything, if only for a short period of time (sugar, cigarettes, alcohol, driving, etc.)? Write about the experience.

Daily Word: Possibilities

THE AUTHOR'S WAY JOURNAL

Today I am Grateful for: _____

THE AUTHOR'S WAY JOURNAL

Day 64   Date: ____/____/____

Write about your proudest accomplishment.

Daily Word: Kindness

THE AUTHOR'S WAY JOURNAL

Today I am Grateful for:

THE AUTHOR'S WAY JOURNAL

Day 65   Date: ____/____/____

Write about a new skill you learned as an adult (painting, writing, skiing, dancing, etc.).

Daily Word: Patience

THE AUTHOR'S WAY JOURNAL

Today I am Grateful for: _____

THE AUTHOR'S WAY JOURNAL

Day 66 Date: ____/____/____

Imagine your childhood home. What do you see when you look out the door?

Daily Word: Appreciation

THE AUTHOR'S WAY JOURNAL

Today I am Grateful for: _____

THE AUTHOR'S WAY JOURNAL

Day 67   Date: ___/___/___

If there were no obstacles, what change would you make in your life.

Daily Word: Celebration

THE AUTHOR'S WAY JOURNAL

Today I am Grateful for: _____

THE AUTHOR'S WAY JOURNAL

Day 68   Date: ____/____/____

Write about a time when you did something selfless.

Daily Word: Determination

THE AUTHOR'S WAY JOURNAL

Today I am Grateful for:

Day 69   Date: ____/____/____

When you were young, what did you want to be when you grew up. Write about what that would have been like or is like.

Daily Word: Inspiration

THE AUTHOR'S WAY JOURNAL

Today I am Grateful for: _____

Day 70   Date: ____/____/____

If you could live anywhere in the world, where would you live?

Daily Word: Loyalty

THE AUTHOR'S WAY JOURNAL

Today I am Grateful for:

THE AUTHOR'S WAY JOURNAL

## Day 71	Date: ____/____/____

Write about what inspires you.

Daily Word: Outstanding

THE AUTHOR'S WAY JOURNAL

Today I am Grateful for: _____

Day 72   Date: ___/___/___

If you could meet anyone, who would it be? What would you talk about?

Daily Word: Strength

THE AUTHOR'S WAY JOURNAL

Today I am Grateful for: _____

THE AUTHOR'S WAY JOURNAL

Day 73   Date: ____/____/____

Write about a time you had to deal with a difficult person or situation.

Daily Word: Vivacious

THE AUTHOR'S WAY JOURNAL

Today I am Grateful for:

THE AUTHOR'S WAY JOURNAL

Day 74   Date: ____/____/____

Write about something that happened that you felt changed your life.

Daily Word: Worthiness

THE AUTHOR'S WAY JOURNAL

Today I am Grateful for: _____

THE AUTHOR'S WAY JOURNAL

Day 75 					Date: ____/____/____

Write about a time when you either experienced or witnessed Karma.

Daily Word: Improvement

THE AUTHOR'S WAY JOURNAL

Today I am Grateful for:

Day 76 Date: ____/____/____

Write about what you think the future will be like. Think about 10, 20, 200 years in the future.

Daily Word: Faith

THE AUTHOR'S WAY JOURNAL

Today I am Grateful for:

Day 77 Date: ___/___/___

Write about a time when you were a leader. Who did you lead? What was the situation? What did you learn?

Daily Word: Acceptance

THE AUTHOR'S WAY JOURNAL

Today I am Grateful for: _____

THE AUTHOR'S WAY JOURNAL

Day 78   Date: ____/____/____

Write about a fear you have that you would like to overcome.

Daily Word: Calmness

THE AUTHOR'S WAY JOURNAL

Today I am Grateful for:

THE AUTHOR'S WAY JOURNAL

Day 79   Date: ____/____/____

Write about your favorite movie.

Daily Word: Confidence

THE AUTHOR'S WAY JOURNAL

Today I am Grateful for: _____

THE AUTHOR'S WAY JOURNAL

Day 80   Date: ____/____/____

Write about what you do to relax. Do you meditate? Do you exercise? Do you binge watch? What else have you find to help you relax?

Daily Word: Energized

THE AUTHOR'S WAY JOURNAL

Today I am Grateful for: _____

Day 81

Date: ____/____/____

Write about a great experience that you had at one of your jobs. What was it about the experience that was so positive?

Daily Word: Benevolence

THE AUTHOR'S WAY JOURNAL

Today I am Grateful for:

Day 82   Date: ___/___/___

Write about a time that you did something you knew you shouldn't have done. What was the result?

Daily Word: Charity

THE AUTHOR'S WAY JOURNAL

Today I am Grateful for: _____

THE AUTHOR'S WAY JOURNAL

Day 83   Date: ____/____/____

Write about where you were 10 years ago.

Daily Word: Hope

THE AUTHOR'S WAY JOURNAL

Today I am Grateful for: _____

THE AUTHOR'S WAY JOURNAL

Day 84 Date: ____/____/____

Write about an idea that you have that you believe would help others.

Daily Word: Nirvana

THE AUTHOR'S WAY JOURNAL

Today I am Grateful for: _____

THE AUTHOR'S WAY JOURNAL

Day 85   Date: ____/____/____

Write about the biggest risk you have ever taken.

Daily Word: Progress

THE AUTHOR'S WAY JOURNAL

Today I am Grateful for:

THE AUTHOR'S WAY JOURNAL

Day 86   Date: ____/____/____

Write about a creative skill you have. How did you learn this skill? How often do you use it?

Daily Word: Reassurance

THE AUTHOR'S WAY JOURNAL

Today I am Grateful for:

THE AUTHOR'S WAY JOURNAL

Day 87 Date: ____/____/____

What was your favorite game to play as a child?

Daily Word: Light-Hearted

THE AUTHOR'S WAY JOURNAL

Today I am Grateful for: _____

THE AUTHOR'S WAY JOURNAL

Day 88   Date: ____/____/____

Write a thank you to someone who did something kind for you.

Daily Word: Consistency

THE AUTHOR'S WAY JOURNAL

Today I am Grateful for: _____

THE AUTHOR'S WAY JOURNAL

Day 89   Date: ____/____/____

Write about a time when you did something very uncomfortable.

Daily Word: Quantum

THE AUTHOR'S WAY JOURNAL

Today I am Grateful for:

THE AUTHOR'S WAY JOURNAL

Day 90 Date: ____/____/____

Write about what you have learned in the past 90 days using this journal.

Daily Word: Ascendence

THE AUTHOR'S WAY JOURNAL

Today I am Grateful for:

CONGRATULATIONS!!

You now have a wonderful collection of stories, situations, thoughts, ideas, and lots of great content. You might even have a book in these pages. Now might be the perfect time to explore pulling all of your stories together and sharing with your colleagues, clients, friends, family, community or even the world.

If you'd like to learn more about how you can do that here are some options.

Join The Writer's Circle: A Community for Authors. This is a supportive community for writers and authors to get feedback, find writing partners, learn new skills and meet others who can support what you do. Use the QR Code below to join or visit: https://www.linkedin.com/groups/14164059/

Register for a complementary Book Writing strategy session with Jennifer Wright. In this session we will discuss your book project, get crystal clear on your goals and your purpose, understand your audience and create a plan to get your book done and published. Use the second QR code to register for the strategy session or visit www.execuwright.com/stratsession

Join The Writer's Circle.

Register for a Strategy Session

Also by Jennifer Wright:

The Author's Way Podcast

Checkout *The Author's Way Podcast: The Journey to Finding Your Voice*. In this podcast, Jennifer features authors, both published and unpublished and they discuss books and the publishing process. New and aspiring authors have the opportunity to learn how other authors have successfully moved past blocks and limiting beliefs, how they got their books into the hands of their readers and many other tips about becoming a successful author.

The podcast is available on iTunes, Spotify and anywhere you listen to your podcasts.

THE AUTHOR'S WAY JOURNAL

Continued from (day#): _____

THE AUTHOR'S WAY JOURNAL

Continued from (day#): _____

THE AUTHOR'S WAY JOURNAL

Continued from (day#): _____

THE AUTHOR'S WAY JOURNAL

Continued from (day#): _____

THE AUTHOR'S WAY JOURNAL

Continued from (day#): _____

THE AUTHOR'S WAY JOURNAL

Continued from (day#): _____

THE AUTHOR'S WAY JOURNAL

Continued from (day#): _____

THE AUTHOR'S WAY JOURNAL

Continued from (day#): _____

THE AUTHOR'S WAY JOURNAL

Continued from (day#): _____

THE AUTHOR'S WAY JOURNAL

Continued from (day#): _____

THE AUTHOR'S WAY JOURNAL

Continued from (day#): _____

THE AUTHOR'S WAY JOURNAL

Continued from (day#): _____

THE AUTHOR'S WAY JOURNAL

Continued from (day#): _____

THE AUTHOR'S WAY JOURNAL

Continued from (day#): _____

THE AUTHOR'S WAY JOURNAL

Continued from (day#): _____

THE AUTHOR'S WAY JOURNAL

Continued from (day#): _____

THE AUTHOR'S WAY JOURNAL

Continued from (day#): _____

THE AUTHOR'S WAY JOURNAL

Continued from (day#): _____

THE AUTHOR'S WAY JOURNAL

Continued from (day#): _____

THE AUTHOR'S WAY JOURNAL

Continued from (day#): _____

THE AUTHOR'S WAY JOURNAL

Continued from (day#): _____

THE AUTHOR'S WAY JOURNAL

Continued from (day#): _____

THE AUTHOR'S WAY JOURNAL

Continued from (day#): _____

www.ingramcontent.com/pod-product-compliance
Lightning Source LLC
Chambersburg PA
CBHW050334010526
44119CB00004B/142